On the Job™

with an

ASTRONOMER
EXPLORER OF THE UNIVERSE

Jake Miller and Jonathan Rubinstein
Illustrated by Susan Gal

BARRON'S

All inquiries should be addressed to:
Barron's Educational Series, Inc.
250 Wireless Boulevard
Hauppauge, NY 11788
http://www.barronseduc.com

Library of Congress Catalog Card No. 2001135077

International Standard Book No. 0-7641-1868-4

Printed in Singapore
9 8 7 6 5 4 3 2 1

ASTRONOMER
EXPLORER OF THE UNIVERSE

Meet Bridgit and Hugo.

They are friends and neighbors.
Together they guide readers
through the exciting world of
various careers.

▪ ▪

In *On the Job with an Astronomer*, Bridgit and Hugo
meet Dr. Barnes and Dr. Kim, two astronomers.
Bridgit and Hugo watch a solar eclipse and visit
an observatory to learn about what it takes to be
an astronomer.

▪ ▪

Table of Contents

CHAPTER 1

A Solar Eclipse

Hugo and Bridgit are sitting in Hugo's front yard, talking about what they want to do today. It's a fine, sunny Saturday.

They aren't the only ones who are taking advantage of the lovely weather. Dr. George Barnes, Hugo's next-door neighbor, is glancing up at the sky and checking his watch.

"What are you looking for?" Bridgit asks.

"You kids came out just in time," says Dr. Barnes. "In just a few minutes, we're going to have a partial solar eclipse—that means the moon is going to pass between the sun and the earth, so that most of the sun gets blocked by the moon."

He invites Bridgit and Hugo to view the eclipse with him.

"Here, we can watch the action through this," Dr. Barnes says, holding what looks like a simple cardboard box. "It's dangerous to look right at the sun, even when its light is blocked by the moon, so I made this special pinhole projection chamber to watch the eclipse with."

One end of the box has a tiny hole in it the size of a pin prick. Light from the sun passes through the hole, and an image appears on a piece of waxed paper on the other side of the box. Dr. Barnes holds the box up so that he and the kids can see the eclipse.

Gradually, even though there isn't a cloud in the sky, it grows dark. Over the next few minutes the kids watch inside the pinhole camera as the silhouette of the moon passes slowly in front of the sun.

"Wow!" exclaims Bridgit. "That's like magic."

"Thousands of years ago, people thought eclipses *were* magic," Dr. Barnes explains. "The Chinese thought that a huge dragon was eating the sun—they used to bang gongs and shoot off fireworks to scare the dragon off. Astronomy has come a long way since then."

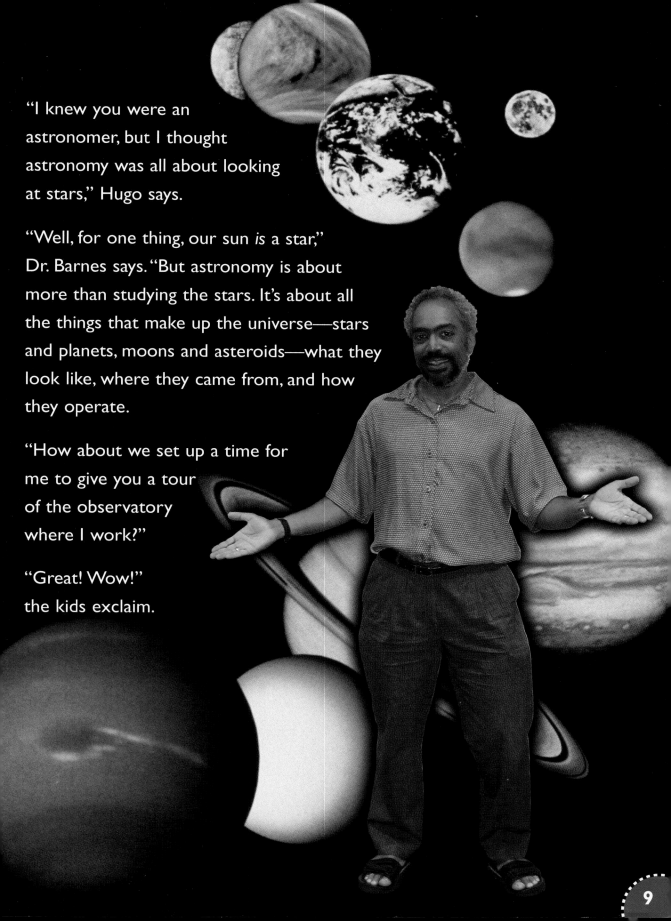

"I knew you were an astronomer, but I thought astronomy was all about looking at stars," Hugo says.

"Well, for one thing, our sun *is* a star," Dr. Barnes says. "But astronomy is about more than studying the stars. It's about all the things that make up the universe—stars and planets, moons and asteroids—what they look like, where they came from, and how they operate.

"How about we set up a time for me to give you a tour of the observatory where I work?"

"Great! Wow!" the kids exclaim.

CHAPTER 2

At the Observatory

A few days later, Bridgit and Hugo arrive at the observatory. Dr. Barnes introduces them to his partner, Dr. Madeleine Kim. The observatory is filled with computers, books, charts, and other gear—and a giant telescope.

Astronomers use telescopes to see things that the ordinary eye can't see alone. The bigger the telescope, the more light can be collected and the more things can be seen. Other kinds of scientists can do experiments, or at least get close enough to their subjects to touch them. But in astronomy, the only way to get information about such far-away subjects is to study the light and other radiation that reaches Earth. Stars are real, physical things that are far away—and big and hot—so they can't be touched or weighed on a scale.

"This thing is huge!" Hugo exclaims.

"We use computers and special electronic cameras to strengthen the images we see, but the size of the telescope is still one of the most important factors. This one isn't even that big; the really huge ones are hundreds of inches across," Dr. Barnes says.

He adjusts the telescope, so that Bridgit and Hugo can look into it.

"What is it you're looking for?" Bridgit asks.

"We can get lots of information from a little bit of light. We can figure out how fast a star is moving, which way it's headed, and whether it has any planets around it. We can even tell what it's made out of just by studying the light we gather in our telescope," Dr. Barnes explains.

"How can you tell what a star is made of?" Bridgit continues.

Dr. Barnes answers, "You've seen a rainbow, right? When you break white light down into the colors it's made of, it's called a *spectrum*. In a star, different kinds of chemicals produce different colors, so a star's spectrum tells us what the star is made of. Knowing what different stars are made of helps us understand how stars are made and what happens to them over the course of their existence."

Dr. Kim says, "Astronomers study everything from nebulae, which are clouds of gas, to black holes, which are the burned-out remains of stars that are so massive not even light can escape the pull of their gravity."

"Astronomers also study things like planets, comets, and asteroids, and even the areas in between stars that look like empty space. As much as we've learned about the universe, there's a great deal we don't yet understand," Dr. Barnes adds.

"Did you know, for example," asks Dr. Kim, "that comets are big balls of ice and dust? They fly through the solar system, rushing by Earth every so often. Some scientists even believe that comets may have deposited the materials onto Earth—like water— that we need to live."

What the Ancients Knew

Long ago, astronomers struggled just to figure out what was happening in the sky they could see with their bare eyes. Ancient peoples built pyramids and other monuments as a way of measuring the movement of the sun and the stars through the sky as the seasons changed.

They imagined that the stars made pictures in the sky, like connect-the-dots, and they gave the pictures names and made up stories about them. Some of these pictures, which we call constellations, are the Little Bear and Leo the Lion.

Some people even believed that they could tell the future by reading secret messages in the constellations. But they also figured out that the stars move according to patterns that we can predict. Once they knew that, they could tell when it was time to plant their crops and how to navigate by the light of the stars.

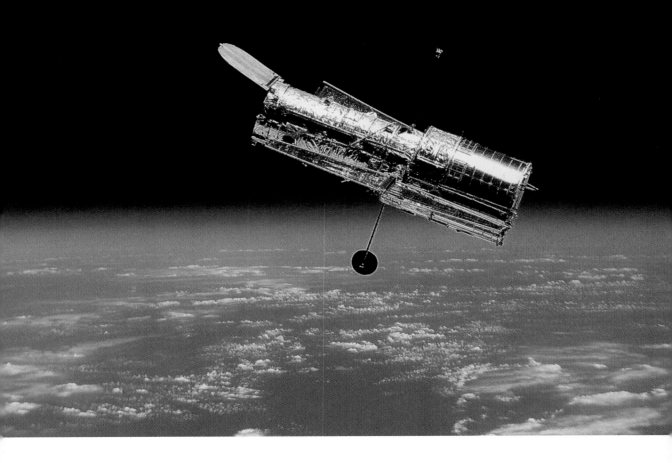

"Over time our telescopes have gotten bigger and better. A lot of observatories are high on mountaintops to get away from city streetlights. Also, the air that we breathe distorts the images we see from space, so the higher up the telescope is, the clearer an image it can make," Dr. Kim says. "We even have telescopes on satellites, like the Hubble space telescope. Since it would be tough for an astronomer to go into space to use the telescope, the satellite beams images back to Earth, which we study down here.

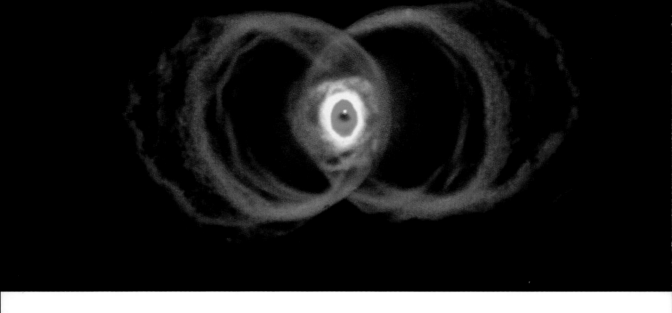

"We also have telescopes that look at radio waves, X rays, and all kinds of other energy," Dr. Kim points out. "They are just different wavelengths of radiation, sort of like colors that we can't see. Since different kinds of objects produce different types of radiation, these various telescopes let us study all kinds of different objects, like pulsars, which are fast-spinning objects that let off flashes of radio waves."

100 billion- that's 100,000,000,000. Really!

"We can also do more complicated calculations, thanks to the invention of more sophisticated mathematics and computers. When you think about the fact that there are probably 100 billion galaxies, and 100 billion stars in each galaxy, that's a lot of numbers to crunch," says Dr. Barnes.

"That's more stars than I can imagine," says Bridgit.

The Sun as Center

For a long time, most people believed that the earth was at the center of the universe, and the sun and the stars all revolved around it. About 500 years ago, an astronomer named Copernicus noticed that what he observed in the sky didn't jibe with that. In trying to do the math to explain how the planetary orbits would work, he realized that the whole system would make more sense if the earth went around the sun.

The idea wasn't popular at first, but a string of great scientists—Tycho Brahe, Johannes Kepler, and Galileo Galilee (who was the first astronomer to use a telescope)—kept working on the theory, doing careful observations and careful math. The modern science of astronomy was born because people saw phenomena in the sky that they wanted to understand, and used observation and mathematics to unravel the mystery.

CHAPTER 3 About the Universe

"Yes, think about how big it all is. There are nine planets in our solar system, and the earth is the third closest to the sun, but the sun is still about 93 million miles away," Dr. Kim says.

"The distances are so vast that astronomers talk about them in light years—that's the distance a flash of light can travel in a year. In 1 second, light can go 186,000 miles—that's seven times around the earth. So in a year, light can go almost 6 trillion miles. That's 6 million times 1 million," says Dr. Barnes.

"Wow, talk about fast!" says Hugo. "But if it takes years and years for the light from distant stars to reach us, then all that information must be old news."

"You're right, Hugo, but that can be a good thing, too. It's almost like having a time machine. With the Hubble space telescope and some of our radio and X-ray telescopes, we can see events that took place millions and millions of years ago when the universe was young, because the radiation from the farthest reaches of space has been traveling for such a long time. In fact, we can see some things that we think are from the beginning of the universe," Dr. Barnes says.

JUPITER

MARS
EARTH
VENUS
MERCURY

SATURN

NEPTUNE PLUT

URANUS

"The beginning of the universe?" Bridgit says. "That's a lot to think about. Do all astronomers have their heads so far out in space?"

"No, Bridgit, some of us like to deal with things that are closer to home," says Dr. Barnes. There are plenty of exciting mysteries to explore in our own tiny corner of our own little galaxy. Some astronomers spend all their time studying the planets in our own solar system."

"There's an advantage to working in the neighborhood, too. We are able to send spacecraft to explore the planets, take close-up pictures, even collect samples of gases from their atmosphere and soils from their surface," Dr. Kim says.

"You mean like the astronauts," Hugo says.

Dr. Kim answers, "Exactly. We send explorers to the moon, and we're hoping to send a crew to Mars. We also send robotic spaceships all over the solar system, which send back fantastic photos and information about all kinds of things. Astronomers constantly study geology and weather patterns, as well as the possibility of life on other planets."

Look Out for the Moon!

The moon changes a lot. It rises about 40 minutes later each night, and moves through different parts of the sky. The moon also has phases; it changes from full moon, to half moon, to new (no) moon, and back again every 28 days. Since the moon is so bright, its location and phases have a big impact on how visible other objects are in the night sky. Knowing when a moonlit or moonless night is coming will help you plan when you want to do some stargazing.

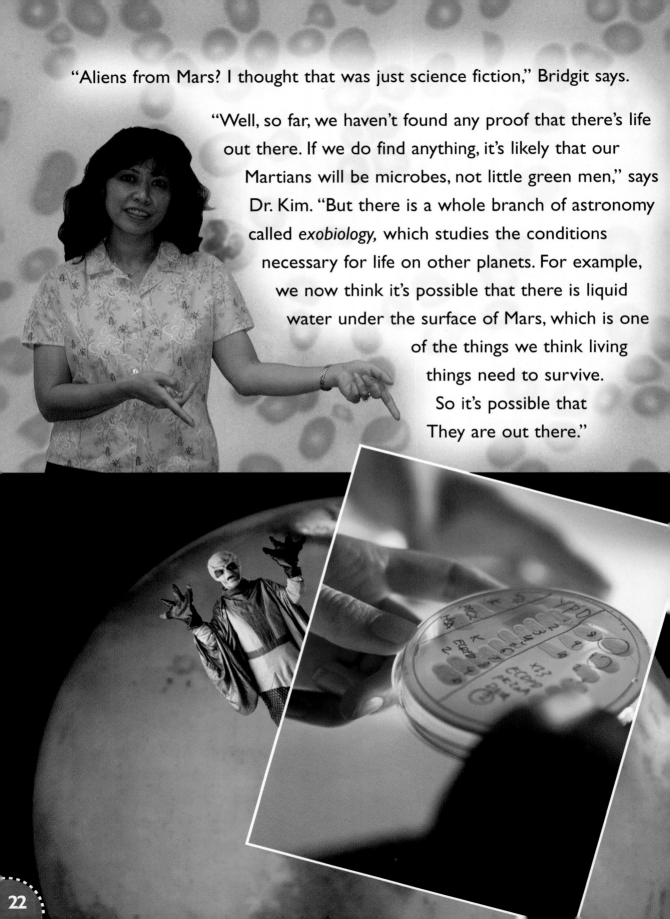

"Aliens from Mars? I thought that was just science fiction," Bridgit says.

"Well, so far, we haven't found any proof that there's life out there. If we do find anything, it's likely that our Martians will be microbes, not little green men," says Dr. Kim. "But there is a whole branch of astronomy called *exobiology,* which studies the conditions necessary for life on other planets. For example, we now think it's possible that there is liquid water under the surface of Mars, which is one of the things we think living things need to survive. So it's possible that They are out there."

We've sent messages into space from some of our spaceships, just in case they run into anyone out there," Dr. Barnes says. "One ship sent recordings of Earth music—including a song by Chuck Berry, a rock-and-roll star from the 1950s—just in case any aliens hearing the music like to swing."

CHAPTER 4

Education and Training

"Microbes, pulsars, light waves—that's a lot to know about," says Hugo. "How did you ever learn so much?"

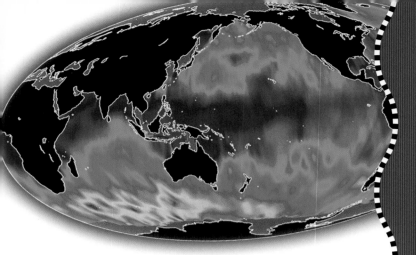

Dr. Kim explains, "Not every astronomer knows about *all* of these things. But there is a lot to know about. We both spent four years in college, and then went back to learn more."

"We studied physics, chemistry, engineering, and mathematics. Some astronomers also study geology and biology," says Dr. Barnes.

News from Space

From outerspace, spaceships and satellites are in a unique position to collect information about planet Earth, helping earthlings live in a better place. For example:

- Equipment on NASA's Terra spacecraft monitors the major sources and movement of air pollution. Terra circles Earth 16 times every day.

- A special camera on board Terra has shot an image of the Atlantic Ocean's Gulf Stream, showing the changing water temperature and the complex interaction of the sea with the atmosphere.

- Satellites regularly map land surfaces, giving us accurate and detailed maps of our cities. These maps show patterns of growth, roadways, and rain runoff.

These results are because of NASA's Earth Science Enterprise, which uses space tools to study how natural and human-induced change affects our global environment.

"We also had to learn to do research on our own," says Dr. Kim. "Learning how to communicate our research is one of the most important parts of the job. We have to write papers and share our discoveries with other astronomers and scientists."

"Once you have a degree in
astronomy, there are all kinds of jobs you can do.
A lot of astronomers work for universities, where they teach classes
in astronomy and physics, and do research. Many astronomers work at
planetariums—domed theaters with light-show exhibits of the solar system—
where they can share their love of science with the widest possible audience.
Other astronomers work at observatories, where they help researchers
collect all sorts of information they need to do their work," Dr. Barnes adds.
"And others help to develop and run the incredible computer systems and
instruments involved with space research.

"Some astronomers work for the National Aeronautics and Space Administration (NASA) or the Jet Propulsion Laboratory (JPL), a government-funded research center that deals with space. Astronomers can also work for private companies. Once you learn how to operate one of these big telescopes, or how to work with satellite and spaceship technology, there are lots of skills you can put to use here on Earth," reports Dr. Barnes.

"But whether you're doing your own research, looking for a brand-new star, teaching a group of young scientists, arranging a light show at a planetarium, or inventing space technology, you still get the thrill of exploring the universe," Dr. Kim says. "It's amazing!"

CHAPTER 5 Saying Good-Bye

It's time for Bridgit and Hugo to leave the observatory and say good-bye to the two astronomers.

"Don't worry kids—the pros don't get to have all the fun. There are plenty of exciting things you can do while you are learning about astronomy. The sky—the universe—is so big, there's always room for discovery. Amateur astronomers, as well as ordinary people and kids, spot all kinds of things before the professionals do, like new asteroids and comets," Dr. Barnes says.

"You don't need a telescope to start looking. A good pair of binoculars is a great way to get started," Dr. Kim said, smiling. "Who knows? You two might team up to find a new comet, and you could name it after yourselves!"

"Yeah, Comet Hugo-Bridgit," Hugo says.

"I was thinking more like Comet Bridgit-Hugo," Bridgit says.

"I guess we have to spot one first!" says Hugo.

"Have fun stargazing," says Dr. Barnes. "And I'll let you know about the next eclipse we can watch together."

Comet Higit! Or how about Brugo?

Activities

Being an astronomer is a creative, challenging job that requires a special set of abilities.

You might be surprised at how many of the most important skills you already have.

- Do you like to look at the stars and imagine what goes on in space?

- Do you like to solve puzzles with just a few clues?

- Do you like to find new ways to look at the world around you?

Try the following activities on your own or with a group of friends, and find out if you have what it takes to be an astronomer.

Night-Sky Log

Start your own log or journal to keep track of your nocturnal observations (that means the things you see at night). Things change quickly in the night sky, so astronomers take careful notes of which stars and planets they have seen, when and where they saw them, and what the conditions were for viewing.

Ask yourself these questions when you are writing in your log:

- What are the weather conditions?

- What time did the sun set (or rise if you are an early riser)?

- Did you see any shooting stars?

- Did you see any other special features in the sky?

Make sure you note where in the sky and when you see all of these things. Were the meteors straight overhead, or were they more toward the north, south, east, or west?

You can also use your star log to write about how sky watching makes you feel, or about what you think life might be like on another planet. Paint a picture of the sunset or draw a sketch of the moonrise. Paste in clippings of photographs from astronomy sites you find on the Internet.

If you need a flashlight to write by, cover a lamp with a sheet of red cellophane, so the light doesn't interfere with your night vision. Also, remember to dress warmly. Find a viewing area away from streetlights and other light sources to make it easier to see faint stars.

That constellation sure looks like a dog!

ACTIVITY 2

Use a Star Chart

Even expert astronomers need help finding their way from star to star. They use star charts something like this one to target their viewing. This chart will work for any night anywhere in the **Northern Hemisphere**, if it's not too cloudy.

The stars pictured on the chart are all found around the *celestial north pole,* an imaginary spot in space located directly over the **North Pole** of planet Earth. As Earth spins through space, rotating around the **North Pole,** these stars spin around celestial north.

Polaris, also called the North Star, is located very near to the celestial north pole. If you look toward the north on a clear night, you should be able to spot the constellations pictured here.

Keep track in your log of the favorite star patterns you sight. Note where in the sky you see them at different times of the year and different times of night. For example, is the Big Dipper to the left or right of, or above or below, the North Star?

Once you have the group shown here mastered, try using a more complete star finder; you can find them for sale in nature stores and bookstores. Computer software programs are also available that combine star charts with night-sky simulators, so you can see what the sky looks like anywhere on Earth on any night.

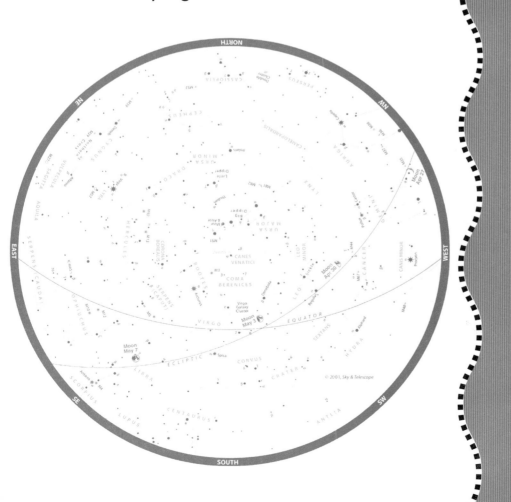

ACTIVITY 3 Star Trails

Try photographing the stars as they move across the sky. The camera records their passage as arcs, little curved lines, which are called *trails*.

You'll need a few simple pieces of equipment:

- a camera with a "bulb" or a "time" setting that lets you keep the shutter open for long periods of time. To avoid using up the camera's batteries, use a manual camera that works without batteries; just make sure that you can take time-exposure pictures with it.

- a tripod to hold your camera steady, so the stars won't jiggle during a long exposure.

- a cable release that lets you trip the shutter button without jostling the camera.

- fast film—ASA 400 and up.

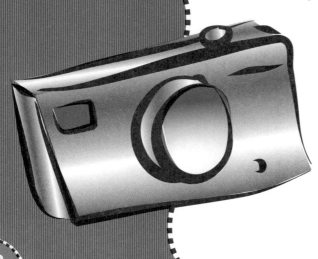

Set your camera on the tripod, pointing at the sky. No tripod? Try setting the camera on a beanbag or soft backpack—anything steady. You can let the camera work on the picture while you have fun sky watching.

Plan to photograph on a very dark, moonless night. When there is light from surrounding streets and homes, the sky in your photograph will turn white and the stars will disappear in exposures longer than a minute or two.

Trip the shutter button and wait. The longer you leave the shutter open, the longer the trails will be. Make sure you wait at least 1 minute.

Experiment with different exposure lengths. In shorter exposures the individual stars will be clearer and you should be able to pick out constellations. If it is extremely dark, you can make exposures for 15 minutes or more, with dramatic star trails.

Photographing stars and other features that astronomers study is called *astro-photography*. It usually requires powerful telescopic cameras that zoom in on a far-away star or other object and computer-controlled motors to turn the telescope as it moves through the sky.

Star Patterns

As the earth moves through space, rotating and revolving around the sun, we see different stars in the night sky. This makes it difficult to memorize a star's position. However, you can memorize the patterns of stars and their relation to each other. People have been finding patterns in the sky and making connect-the-dots pictures out of them for thousands of years.

Before you try to memorize any of these well-known patterns, which are known as *constellations,* look at the stars and make up some of your own. Try sketching the pictures in your log.

Here's a little-known fact: The Big Dipper is not a constellation, but only part of the constellation Ursa Major, the Large Bear. It is called an *asterism.*

Planet Search

Besides the sun and the moon, some of the brightest spots in the night sky aren't stars at all—they're planets. One way to help tell planets from stars is that they emit steadier light—they twinkle less.

You can see four of the brightest planets— Jupiter, Saturn, Venus, and Mars—with the naked eye, if you know where to look.

Check with your local planetarium or astronomy club, look in a current astronomy magazine or book, or check the Internet for precise information about when and where to spot our solar system neighbors.

Dogs are from Pluto.

ACTIVITY 6

Solar System Map

Real planets have orbits that aren't perfect circles—they're stretched-out ovals called *ellipses*. But this chart will give you a good idea of the distance between the planets.

Make a map of our solar system. To get an idea of how far apart things are in space, get a piece of paper that's at least 40 inches long. The width of the paper isn't important. If you can't find a piece that long, tape a few pieces together. You will also need a pencil or pen, drawing compass, ruler, pin, and piece of string 40 inches or longer. On this scale, 1 inch equals 1 astronomical unit, which is about 93 million miles, the distance of the earth from the sun.

- Make a dot in the center of the left edge of the paper to represent the sun, which is at the center of the solar system. Your map will only show a segment of each planetary orbit you draw.

- Using the compass, draw half a circle with a $\frac{1}{2}$-inch radius. That's the orbit of Mercury.

- Use the compass to make orbits for Venus ($\frac{3}{4}$ inch), Earth (1 inch), and Mars ($1\frac{1}{2}$ inches). The rest of the orbits will be too big to use the compass, so use the string instead.

- Pin one end of the string to the sun, and use the string compass to make orbits for Jupiter ($5\frac{1}{4}$ inches), Saturn ($9\frac{1}{2}$ inches), Uranus ($19\frac{1}{4}$ inches), Neptune (30 inches), and Pluto ($39\frac{1}{2}$ inches).

If you were to include the next nearest star (Proxima Centauri, 4.24 light years away) on the same map, you would need a piece of paper that was more than 273,000 inches long—that's about 4.3 miles.

A *meteor* is a tiny particle of dust that burns up when it falls from space into Earth's atmosphere. If the object is large enough to remain intact until it hits the ground, it's called a *meteorite*.

Watch a Falling Star

The bright, flashing lights we see shooting across the sky are called *falling stars* and *shooting stars*. But they aren't stars at all; they're meteors.

The best periods to view meteors are when Earth is orbiting through a particularly dusty region of the solar system. Some of the best meteor showers are the Perseids (which peak around August 12), the Quadrantids (January 3), the Delta-Aquaris (July 29), and the Leonids (November 17). Around these dates, the best hours to watch the sky are from midnight to about 4 o'clock in the morning, when some showers may rain more than 100 meteors per hour.

Sky Watch

If you decide you want to get serious about sky watching, but you're not ready yet to have your own telescope, binoculars are a great way to get started. Experts recommend 7×50 binoculars—7× refers to magnification power and 50 refers to the diameter of the light-gathering lens. Bigger lenses gather more light but are very heavy.

One of the best ways to use your binoculars is to sit in a reclining position in a comfortable garden chair, resting your elbows on the arms. With binoculars, you will be able to see five times as many stars as you can with your naked eyes, plus the craters of the moon, the rings of Saturn, and a host of other fascinating subjects.

Glossary

Comet
A frozen ball of dust and ice that orbits the sun. Solar radiation causes dust and ice particles to form a tail that always points away from the sun.

Constellation
A group of stars whose outline forms a person, creature, or object, like Orion or Leo the Lion. Astronomers use constellations to find their way in the night sky.

Exobiology
A field of astronomy that studies the possibility of life on other planets by looking for evidence of the conditions necessary for life.

Galaxy
Throughout the universe, most stars seem to bunch together in large groups known as galaxies. Our galaxy, called the Milky Way, is shaped like a spiral, and contains 200 billion stars, plus huge clouds of gas. Other galaxies are shaped like ellipses and cigars, while some seem to have no particular shape at all.

Meteor
A particle of dust that burns up in the earth's atmosphere, creating a "shooting star."

Satellite
An object that circles another object in space, held in place by gravity. The moon is a natural satellite that circles the earth. There are also many human-made satellites, like the Hubble space telescope.

Spectrum
When visible light is broken down into its component parts, it forms a rainbow or spectrum. The full radiation spectrum includes "colors" that we can't see, including infrared and ultraviolet, X rays, microwaves, and radio waves. These different kinds of energy provide valuable information for astronomers.

Resources

Careers in Astronomy

American Astronomical Society
Education Office
University of Chicago
5640 South Ellis Avenue
Chicago IL 60367

Sky Watching

David H. Levy
Skywatching
New York: Time-Life, 2000

Chet Raymo
365 Starry Nights: An Introduction to Astronomy for Every Night of the Year
New York: Simon and Schuster, 1992

H.A. Rey
The Stars: A New Way to See Them
Boston: Houghton Mifflin, 1997

About the Universe

Stephen Hawkings
A Brief History of Time
New York: Bantam Books, 1998

Kristin Lippincott
Astronomy (Eyewitness Guides)
New York: DK Publishing, 2000

Seymour Simon
Universe
New York: Harper Trophy, 2000

Paul P. Sipiera and Dennis Brindell Fradin
Black Holes
New York: Children's Press, 1997

Biographies

Claire L. Datnow
Edwin Hubble: Discoverer of Galaxies
Berkeley Heights, N.J.: Enslow, 2001

James MacLachlan
Galileo Galilei: First Physicist
New York: Oxford University Press, 1999

Astronomy Software

Starry Night (star chart and astronomy simulator software)
Toronto: Space.com, 2000

Internet Sites

http://www.aavso.org/
for star charts

http://www.chabotspace.org/
for astronomy kid stuff

http://www.jpl.nasa.gov/
for the main Jet Propulsion Lab address

http;//pds.jpl.nasa.gov/planets/
for images of the planets in our solar system

http://kids.msfc.nasa.gov/
for kids 13 and younger

http://liftoff.msfc.nasa.gov/
for kids 13 and older

http://www.nasa.gov/
for the main NASA address

http://nix.nasa.gov/
for planetary videos and photos

The books in this series are produced by Orange Avenue, Inc.
Creative Director: Hallie Warshaw
Writer: Jonathan Rubinstein
Contributing Writer: Jake Miller
Design & Production: Britt Menendez, B Designs
Illustrator: Susan Gal
Editor: Robyn Brode
Photographer: Emily Vassos
Creative Assistant: Emily Vassos

Models: Gibor Basri, professor of astronomy at the University of California, Berkeley, and Alice Liwanig

Special Thanks to: Alan Scribner, Steve Nightingale, Wilford French, and Tammy Bosler; and Chabot Space & Science Center and Judyth Colin for allowing us to take photographs at their beautiful facility

Photo Credits: American Association of Variable Star Observers (AAVSO), Corbis, Eyewire, NASA Image Exchange, Photo Disc, and Picture Quest